CHANGE YOUR POSTURE!
CHANGE YOUR Life!

AFFIRMATION JOURNAL
Volume 10 — Humility

D NICOLE WILLIAMS

Sh'Shares NETWORK
www.ShShares.com

CHANGE YOUR POSTURE! CHANGE YOUR LIFE!
AFFIRMATION JOURNAL

Volume 10 — Humility

Copyright © 2016 by D Nicole Williams

All rights reserved. No portion of this publication may be reproduced, distributed, or transmitted in any form or by any means, including photocopying, recording, or other electronic or mechanical methods, without the prior written permission of the publisher, except in the case of brief quotations embodied in critical reviews and certain other noncommercial uses permitted by copyright law.

For permission requests, write to the publisher, addressed
"ATTN: Permissions" at the following:

Sh'Shares NETWORK, LLC
1601-1 N Main Street 13202
Jacksonville, FL 32206-0202
www.ShShares.com

Bulk discounts are available on quantity purchases by associations, corporations, and others for business, educational and ministry use. For details, contact the publisher at the address above.

Library of Congress Control Number: 2016918044

ISBN: 978-1-942650-36-2

```
VOL. 01: 978-1-942650-27-0 (Journal, Faithfulness)
VOL. 02: 978-1-942650-28-7 (Journal, Joy)
VOL. 03: 978-1-942650-29-4 (Journal, Peace)
VOL. 04: 978-1-942650-30-0 (Journal, Wisdom)
VOL. 05: 978-1-942650-31-7 (Journal, Diligence)
VOL. 06: 978-1-942650-32-4 (Journal, Self-Control)
VOL. 07: 978-1-942650-33-1 (Journal, Goodness)
VOL. 08: 978-1-942650-34-8 (Journal, Patience)
VOL. 09: 978-1-942650-35-5 (Journal, Gentleness)
VOL. 11: 978-1-942650-37-9 (Journal, Kindness)
VOL. 12: 978-1-942650-38-6 (Journal, Love)
```

Printed in the United States of America
FIRST EDITION

Humility

Posture 03. Passion for OTHERS
  10. Humility

01.	I Will Work on HUMILITY!	8
02.	I Will SACRIFICE!	11
03.	I Will Not Fear OPPORTUNITY!	12
04.	I Will Not Be ASHAMED!	13
05.	I Am LISTENING!	14
06.	I Am a LEADER!	15
07.	I Will Be a GREAT Example!	16
08.	I Am a TEACHER!	18
09.	My Life is An EXAMPLE!	20
10.	I Will PRACTICE What I Teach!	21
11.	I Am THANKFUL for Support!	22
12.	I Will Not Fear GREATNESS!	22
13.	I Will HONOR My Friends!	24
14.	I Will CHERISH Friendship!	25
15.	I Will HONOR My Family!	26
16.	I Will CHERISH Family!	27
17.	I Will CHERISH Others!	30
18.	I Will CHERISH Diversity!	32
19.	I Will Seek Out Others for Constructive Feedback!	33
20.	I Will HONOR My Mentors!	36
21.	I Will Value SELF-EXAMINATION!	38
22.	I Will HUMBLE Myself!	39
23.	I Will HONOR My Parents!	40
24.	I Will Look to Others for HELP!	42
25.	I Will LISTEN!	43
26.	I Will LISTEN with My WHOLE Heart!	44
27.	I Will Consistently Support an Entrepreneur!	46
28.	I Will Consistently Support a Worthy Cause!	48
29.	I Will CHERISH Growth!	50
30.	I Will Be BETTER!	51
31.	I Will Be HUMBLE!	52

introduction

Greetings Dear Friends!

Welcome to this beloved journey toward increased humility in life. Humility is a tough one. The activity of humility is not so tough, but what is noticeably difficult are our responses to reminders that we may not be as humble as we'd like. Life presents us with opportunities to be more humble daily. Are we taking advantage of them as we should? Well, this journal will surely help us to figure it out!

As you work through this journal, share your progress along the way. You can email SHINE@change-your-posture.com with your news! I would LOVE to hear of your hopes, helps, and hiccups, so keep me posted!!!

Talk to you soon!
— Coach D!

How to Get the MOST Out of This Journal…

★ **Read. Write. Reflect.**

★ **Cry** …*if you need to…*

★ **Phone a friend and let's get major WORK done in our lives with these journals!!!**

Take the time you need to be the friend YOU need. Do it for YOU! Don't wait around for another! This is the season to take over your own life and take control of your thoughts through affirmation!

★ **Thought bubbles are included throughout the book so you can share your own ideas and reflections.**

★ **There are boxes included for you to doodle OR you can use them as spaces to ask questions of yourself… that's up to you!**

No matter what you use each space for, be sure that you are authentic! This is *your* time, and this is *your* space to be the YOU that YOU need for YOU! Do it *now*. Show YOURSELF what YOU are made of…

Change Your Posture! Change Your LIFE!

Humility

POSTURE 03 : *PASSION* FOR OTHERS

01 Humility

"
I Will Work on HUMILITY!
"

Our lives don't exist simply for the betterment of ourselves. By the same token, the people around us have MUCH to bring into our lives if we position ourselves to receive their blessed abundance.

In this season, we shift our focal point to people. We focus on being respectable humans as we coexist alongside others. Repositioning ourselves for growth requires *constant* concentration on humility. Humility affords us with a disposition best suited for giving and receiving—activities that increase our awareness of charitable equity within all humanity.

Humility Affirmation *(Repeat this aloud)*

Through humility, I have the courage to be selfless—I think of myself less. Humility shows my bravery, reverence and wisdom. I confront fear and doubt while refraining from despair. Humility is how I teach in love by faithfulness.

This month highlights the importance of humility within our lives by showing the roles we must take on *for* ourselves *toward* others. In humbly serving others, we morally sharpen ourselves while increasing our personal and professional value, our vitality and our longevity.

Say Aloud: I Will Work on Humility! I Will Increase My Value!

Journal Prompt...
What current practices of mine show a great measure of humility?

_____
_____
_____

How can I show even more humility in all aspects of life?

_____
_____
_____

JournalPrompt...

Do I allow humility in my life? ____   **What does that look like?** _____

_____
_____
_____
_____

Do I allow service in my life? ____   **What does that look like?** _____

_____
_____
_____

What are my humility issues?

_____
_____
_____
_____

What are my issues with serving others?

_____
_____
_____
_____

How can I resolve these issues?

_____
_____
_____
_____

Prayer of Humility

Compose a dedicated *Prayer of Humility* that you will commit to this month.

Consider the areas of life where you could be humble. If you get stuck, use the prompts on the previous page to fill in the blanks. Fill the entire page with your humility prayer.

Print it. Post it. Read it daily.

Humility

" I Will SACRIFICE! "

Changes often come through much rigor and strife, the combination of which could be quickly summed up as sacrifice. Changes are often seen as sacrifice because adjustments aren't always wanted or even *needed* at times. Life is all about sacrifice—it's about making constant credible changes on a progressive continuum toward GREATNESS!

Success in life *requires* change—constant change—change that mandates humble sacrifice to see its reward. If you are to see the end results that you dream of, sacrifice should be constant and comfortable enough for you to remove any negative response that you have toward it. In fact, you should WELCOME sacrifice! Sacrificing means that you're humbly asserting yourself toward compelling growth.

Affirmation Journal

★ How do I feel about making sacrifices for myself?

_____

_____

_____

★ How often do I practice making sacrifices for myself?

_____

_____

_____

★ How do my lifelong sacrifices play into my future?

_____

_____

_____

Say Aloud: I Will Sacrifice! Sacrifice Makes Me Better!

Sacrifice is a part of life. It's supposed to be.
It's not something to regret. It's something to aspire to.

MITCH ALBOM

POSTURE 03 : *PASSION* FOR OTHERS

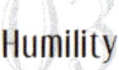

Humility

"

I Will Not Fear OPPORTUNITY!

"

Opportunity abounds in life. Like love, and God, opportunity is everywhere and in ALL things. Opportunity is yours to find, yet you will NEVER be able to see opportunity through blinders of fear!

Affirmation Journal

★ How do I feel about opportunity?

_____
_____
_____

★ How do I feel about fear?

_____
_____
_____

★ How does fear impact opportunities that come my way?

_____
_____
_____

Fear is stifling! It stands in the way of success based on your inability to see opportunity. You can't *seize* what you can't *see*! Goals, and the attainment of dreams, ride on your ability to take advantage of opportunities that come your way daily. Ambitions can't be limited only to what you can create for yourself. You must be willing to see opportunity in *all* things and also be ambitious enough to subsequently create the life that you desire using the advancements presented to you. You can't see GRAND levels of success if you succumb to the boundaries of fear. The magnitude of your goals must always trump that of your fears!

Create goals that are powerful! Don't let fear impede your progress!

Say Aloud: **I Will Not Fear Opportunity! I Will Not Fear!!!**

Humility

> # I Will Not Be ASHAMED!

Success can't be had without failure, and you can't learn from failure without embracing it. If you can't accept your mistakes, you can't learn from them, and if you can't learn, you can't teach. In that way, you make no progress at all!

Say Aloud: **I Will Not Be Ashamed! I Will Hold My Head High!**

People are more afraid of losing than they are of winning. The fear of losing is so great that people don't even *try*, so they lose EVERY single time! There is no success without much failure! Success isn't found by what is gained in the end—success is found along the path toward attainment:

"You know, Charlie Brown,
they say we learn more from losing than from winning."

— LINUS VAN PELT

Failure is nothing to be ashamed of, so fail FORWARD with your head held HIGH and with the world at your feet! Be PROUD of the progress you've made understanding that failure is to be expected, AND appreciated, along the way!

A man should never be ashamed to own that he has been in the wrong,
which is but saying in other words that he is wiser today than he was yesterday.

— ALEXANDER POPE

Journal Prompt...

What pains have I faced regarding shame?

1. _____
2. _____
3. _____

What pains have I faced regarding regret?

1. _____
2. _____
3. _____

How can I have a better outcome and MAKE the BEST of life?

_____
_____
_____

POSTURE 03 : *PASSION* FOR OTHERS

05 Humility

"
I Am LISTENING!
"

Good listening is a skill very difficult to come by. Therefore, it's also difficult to master. Interestingly, there are a number of highly esteemed traits of success that could stand in the way of maintaining a productive listening ear. If you aren't proactive about keeping your ears meek and attentive, traits such as independence, decisiveness, prowess and more, could stand in the way of more effortless success found through acute listening.

Listening is a never-ending process—it NEVER stops. Listening involves much more than just your ears, so be proactive in listening even when you aren't *hearing* what is being said.

Exceptional listening requires full mental, emotional and spiritual participation which includes the involvement of your senses, your experiences and your personal awareness.

Affirmation Journal

★ **How effective am I at listening?**

_____
_____
_____
_____
_____
_____
_____

★ **How can I be better at listening?**

_____
_____
_____
_____
_____
_____

HUMILITY

★ Why is it important for me to become a better listener?

_____
_____
_____
_____
_____
_____

Say Aloud: I Am Listening! I Listen with My Senses and Skills!

---

06 Humility

" **I Am a LEADER!** "

YOU Are a LEADER!

You are a trailblazer! Once you realize the extent of your POWER as a tastemaker, channel that energy into profitable endeavors that further drive progressive enterprise! Let your leadership skill be evident in ALL that your hands touch! Let your thoughts, dreams and visions inspire others to *be* and to *do* their BEST!

Say Aloud: I Am a Leader! I Inspire Others to *Be* the BEST!

It's EXCITING to be an inspiration, a role model, a mentor, a leader, an exhorter or a COACH! It's EXCITING to help others achieve goals, dreams and business success!!! Find out what makes YOU excited about being a leader and do THAT! Do it richly and lovingly, with pride, and in competence. Be excited about imparting your knowledge to others using actionable means. No matter how far your progress as a leader, always, always, ALWAYS remain COMPLETELY humble!

> *The challenge of leadership is to be strong, but not rude;*
> *be kind, but not weak; be bold, but not bully;*
> *be thoughtful, but not lazy; be humble, but not timid;*
> *be proud, but not arrogant;*
> *have humor, but without folly.*
>
> JIM ROHN

Humility

> ## I Will Be a GREAT Example!

Great leadership is found in great stewardship—the BEST leaders lead *themselves* first! They show command of leadership through how they purportedly guide their own lives. True leaders don't have to be formally asked to take positions of leadership—they default to head roles without specific instruction to do so. The lifestyle of a leader demonstrates fitness for authoritative roles through influential stewardship.

Affirmation Journal

★ How great of an example am I?

_____
_____
_____
_____
_____
_____
_____
_____

★ What does my lifestyle exemplify to others?

_____
_____
_____
_____
_____
_____

HUMILITY

★ **How do I show leadership within my example?**

_____
_____
_____
_____
_____
_____
_____
_____
_____
_____

Let your lifestyle lead others onto *right* paths. Be a worthy example of success, perseverance and happiness in the face of all opportunity. Be humble in your efforts and in your presentation of yourself while being BOLD enough to inspire compelling courage within others. Don't be afraid to show the world what you're made of! Be a fine example. Lead with an upright lifestyle that boasts wholeness.

Say Aloud: **I Will Be a Great Example! I Will** *Show* **Leadership!**

POSTURE 03 : *PASSION FOR OTHERS*

08 Humility

> # I Am a TEACHER!

Most people are masters of *telling*. They are masters of directing. They have ALL the best advice to give because they know what EVERYONE else is doing *wrong*. There are entirely too many people who are unafraid to share these unsolicited, misguided opinions. This means trouble!

Instead of freely *telling* so much, be a master of *showing*. The GREAT examples that you find in life are those who are masters of *doing*. They are the people who you never have to *ask* what they are doing—anything that they do is always very readily apparent, without question. Be one of those. Be the type of person who doesn't just *talk*—be a person who *does*. Teach others by the way that you *live*. Teach others by the way that you *show*. Teach others by the way that you DO.

★ You are a teacher!

Affirmation Journal

★ **Am I a master of telling OR Am I a master of doing? How OR Why?**

_____
_____
_____
_____
_____
_____
_____

★ **How well do I teach others by my own actions?**

_____
_____
_____
_____
_____
_____
_____

HUMILITY

★ How can I be better at teaching by example?

_____
_____
_____
_____
_____
_____
_____

Say Aloud: I Am a Teacher! I Teach by Showing and Doing!

*The mediocre teacher tells. The good teacher explains.
The superior teacher demonstrates.
The great teacher inspires.*

WILLIAM ARTHUR WARD

POSTURE 03 : *PASSION* FOR OTHERS

Humility

> ## My Life is an EXAMPLE!

Is your life a good example to others? Are you proud of all you have to offer? Do you share your gifts with others regardless of their willingness to receive? How great are you at stewardship?

These questions, and others, will help you measure your level of unspoken leadership within your circles. If you're unafraid to be who you are, and if you readily show yourself as an effective manager of *yourself*, you're already in place to effectively lead and guide others. Your example of goodness is already apparent through the way that you guide your own actions.

Shared life experiences benefit others who might someday decide to partake in similar journeys as yours. Even without someone else taking the exact route as yours, your personal courage motivates them to be great in their individual aspirations, so how great of an example are you?

Affirmation Journal

★ **What type of example do others see in me?**

_____
_____
_____
_____
_____
_____

★ **How great am I at stewardship?**

_____
_____
_____
_____
_____
_____
_____

★ How can I become a better example?

_____
_____
_____
_____
_____
_____
_____

Say Aloud: My Life is An Example! I Share Life with Others!

---

10 Humility

" I Will PRACTICE What I Teach! "

When viewing your life, others learn from your example. If you demonstrate positive traits, positivity is what they gain. If you demonstrate negative traits, negativity is what they gain. Through simply observing your life, there are those within your environment who eventually become pupils of what you have to teach. Through your teachings, you express your take on life based on your personal experience on a number of topics. Using various methods, you deliver to them what you have to give in the form of solicited and unsolicited advice.

Ask yourself, **"In all of my advising, am I _learning_? Am I making use of the teachings that I dole out to others?"**

Are you? Are you using what you have on yourself first? Is all of your teaching falling—lost on your own deaf ears?

To be a GREAT leader, lead by example—practice what you teach. Don't be so big on advising that you forget to test theories on yourself first. You are your own best pupil!

Say Aloud: I Will Practice What I Teach and Lead by Example!

The way to get started is to quit talking and begin doing.

WALT DISNEY COMPANY

POSTURE 03 : *PASSION* FOR OTHERS

11
Humility

"
I Am THANKFUL for Support!
"

The best support you EVER receive is the support you didn't ask for! Support—no matter the shape, size or format—should always be sincerely appreciated and equally rendered as much as possible. Don't support only those who support your or only those who you *want* to support. Put pride to the side and support others because it's the RIGHT thing to do!

Sometimes, great support seems as hard to come by as great workers. *(This is especially true if you'd like that support to be great workers!* ☺*)* Support, through *any* means, is ALWAYS to be praised and acknowledged! Be thankful for all that's been afforded to you by way of friends, family members, associates and even strangers who've gone the extra mile to help you! Show them how grateful you are and welcome their support well into the future.

Say Aloud: **I Am Thankful for Support!**

Many times, you don't *have* support because you don't *see* support in all of the many ways that it presents itself. Don't overlook what's already being readily given to you. You may be looking in the wrong places for what you already have in sincere abundance! Be humble and be grateful for what you have. Thank others for supporting you!

12
Humility

"
I Will Not Fear GREATNESS!
"

The entrepreneurially minded will NEVER be content with working on someone else's job! Leaders don't remain followers for long. Those aiming for GREATNESS feel anxious amidst mediocrity. Whatever *your* brand of courage,

DO NOT FEAR!!!

HUMILITY

Don't fear the GREATNESS within you, and don't fear the greatness of those around you! Let NOTHING about success intimidate you—be MOTIVATED by it! Be encouraged by progress and by new ways of thinking! Don't settle for mediocrity! Don't pick up mediocre habits and accept them as yours. Rid yourself of self-imposed limits, and be *free* in the knowledge that you're as GREAT as you *think* yourself to be!

Affirmation Journal

★ How great am I? How great can I be?

★ What scares me about greatness?

★ What are my self-imposed limits?

Say Aloud: I Will Not Fear Greatness! I *AM* GREATNESS!

Have no fear of perfection—you'll never reach it.

SALVADOR DALÍ

POSTURE 03 : *PASSION* FOR OTHERS

13 Humility

"
I Will HONOR My Friends!
"

Friends are lifelong companions. Whether close to them in distance or in emotion, friends are lifelong support systems. They are the people you talk to when you tire of talking to yourself. When friends aren't around, you miss their presence because you enjoy having someone to share your life with—your life feels empty without them.

Through honoring friends, you show them the love and appreciation that you have for them. As much as they mean to you, friends should ALWAYS be reminded of the joy they bring! Friendships are your practice field for self-expression, communication and healthy display of feelings. In consideration of all they do for you, your friends should KNOW that they are one of the highlights of your life! This should be evident through how you honor and respect them.

Affirmation Journal

★ How well do I respect my friends?

_____

_____

_____

★ How do I show my friends that I appreciate and admire them?

_____

_____

_____

★ What can I do regularly to show honor to my friends?

_____

_____

_____

Appreciation for your friends should go without saying. This isn't to say that appreciation shouldn't be shown.

Honor your friends—*show* them your love!

Humility

> # I Will CHERISH Friendship!

Friends are the brothers and sisters that you have the grand fortune of choosing! They are your saving grace, your sounding board, your sidekicks and your BRAINS—friends are partners! Friends are one of the most cherished accomplishments you will ever have in life, yet you don't always let 'em know!

Friends are your reminder that you made it—they help you celebrate all that you are and all that you will come to be! Friends keep you honest. They help you live the BEST life! When life doesn't go as planned, friends are there to help you clean up the mess and move forward with dignity!

What would you do without friends?! You might've stayed out of some trouble if it weren't for your friends, but that would give you less stories to tell and far less laughs to share!

Remember ALL that your friends have been for you.

Cherish the joy that they bring into your life!

Affirmation Journal

★ **What do my friends mean to me?**

_____
_____
_____
_____

★ **How have my friends added to the joy of my life?**

_____
_____
_____
_____

Don't walk behind me; I may not lead.
Don't walk in front of me; I may not follow.
Just walk beside me and be my friend.

ALBERT CAMUS

POSTURE 03 : *PASSION* FOR OTHERS

Humility

> # I Will HONOR My Family!

Families are your lifelong support system. Whether you want them to or not, they stick by you through thick and thin. Through your family, you find your initial identity. You formulate your foundational outlook on life based on familial interactions. There is much about your internal and external make-up that you owe directly to your family. Your family is the great foundational measure through which you assess your past and launch your future. For this and more, show them honor.

Your family is honored in how you carry yourself and by how you serve your community and others. You honor your family through your values and exhibitions of solid moral character. Honor toward your family is shown through awareness of family history, linkages and continued connections to loved ones. You honor your family by raising a family of your own that you can be proud of as you share stories passed down through the generations to come.

Say Aloud: I Will Honor My Family!

Affirmation Journal

★ Why is it important to honor my family?

_____
_____
_____
_____
_____
_____

★ In what ways do I show honor to my family?

_____
_____
_____
_____
_____

★ How can I be better about honoring my family?

___

16 Humility

> ## I Will CHERISH Family!

Cherish your family because of your personal make up. Your family helps to mold and shape you into who you are as an individual. They are your listening ears who serve as mirrors into your soul. Many fantastic things can be said about your family and what each individual member is for you. In gratitude, cherish your family for being your first friends and for being the most dependable builders of your character.

Families best teach most things you know about the world!

Today's To-Do's...
★ List the 10 family members that you most cherish.
★ Through the remainder of this month, contact each of these family members.
★ Let each of them know exactly what they mean to you.
★ RECOMMENDATION: Compose a hand-written letter to be delivered to each of them. Mail the letters.
★ Include an envelope and postage within each letter in hopes that your family members write to you in return.

Say Aloud: I Will Cherish My Family!

When everything goes to hell, the people who stand by you, without flinching—they are your family.

JIM BUTCHER

POSTURE 03 : *PASSION* FOR OTHERS

Family Values

Use this listing to record the 10 family members you cherish the most.

Think of all the wonderful things you want to share with them. Commit to sharing your thoughts with each person this month via personal, handwritten letter and declare: I CHERISH My FAMILY!!!

10 Family Members I Cherish
1.   I Cherish You because :
2.   I Cherish You because :
3.   I Cherish You because :
4.   I Cherish You because :
5.   I Cherish You because :

6.

   I Cherish You because :

7.

   I Cherish You because :

8.

   I Cherish You because :

9.

   I Cherish You because :

10.

   I Cherish You because :

POSTURE 03 : *PASSION* FOR OTHERS

17

Humility

" I Will CHERISH Others! "

You don't have to grow through the same experiences as others to value what they've been through. You don't have to encounter the same situations as others to accept their lives. All you need is respect for them as human beings in order to appreciate what others have to offer. The value in others can easily be assessed by a simple review of your own life. Despite language, societal and racial barriers, *everyone* shares similar experiences through generations cross culturally.

Appreciation for another comes from a deep-seated respect for *yourself*. You may not wear the same clothes, have the same lifestyle or even speak the same tongue, but each person shares some similar life experience as you. You don't have to walk a mile in another's shoes to know their pain—your own feet hurt much the same. *Everyone* feels emotions. *Everyone* has pains, and *everyone* seeks love!

Cherish the people around you—not because of what they have to give. Cherish them simply for who they are.

Say Aloud: **I Will Cherish Others! I Respect Their Experience!**

Put My Cherish on TOP!

Use this listing to record the 5 people around you whom you cherish the most.

Think of all the wonderful things you want to share with them. Share your thoughts with each person this month via personal, handwritten letter. Let them know where your CHERISH is!

5 People I Most Cherish

1.

   I Cherish You because :

2.

   I Cherish You because :

3.

   I Cherish You because :

4.

   I Cherish You because :

5.

   I Cherish You because :

POSTURE 03 : *PASSION* FOR OTHERS

18 Humility

> # I Will CHERISH Diversity!

Life presents an ENDLESS spectrum of creativity in the variety of diversification that you are blessed to behold! Through color, culture and creed you have the grand fortune of learning in a number of ways by intermingling your unique frameworks with the diversity of others.

Diversity broadens the horizons of all participants through the platform of inclusion. Newness is welcomed and accepted with the goal of blended growth. Lack of diversity imposes limits on all since there is no new gain in old insights without a varied vantage points. Rules, because of the limits they create, commonly stifle creative variety, diversity of thought and diversity of approach. In diversity, everyone brings their own voice, their own thought process and their own methodology to the table.

There are no rules within diversity, so it is LIMITLESS—without walls, without structure and without boundaries. This makes the possibilities ENDLESS!

Say Aloud: I Will Cherish Diversity!

*Christian, Jew, Muslim, shaman, Zoroastrian,
stone, ground, mountain, river,
each has a secret way of being with the mystery,
unique and not to be judged.*

RUMI

Humility

" I Will Seek Out Others for Constructive Feedback! "

When requesting feedback for growth, it's wise to ask not only those closest to you, but also those who challenge you—both currently and within your chosen future.

One aspect of my certification to become a Life Coach Trainer required that I petition others for feedback. I received GREAT feedback! It was ALL positive! I had to delve deeper to find feedback that would help me to solidify the great output that I was already receiving. I asked for specifics that would help me to *improve*: **Actionable Feedback!**

Regularly Request Feedback from At Least Five Others

- ★ **If you are married or dating, ask your mate.**
- ★ **If you are a parent, ask your child(ren).**
- ★ **If you are an entrepreneur, ask a new client and an old client. Ask your worst—yes, WORST—and best clients.**
- ★ **If you are a student, ask a teacher. If you are a college student, ask someone in the field you aspire to.**
- ★ **Ask someone who has known you for your entire life, and ask someone you just met.**
- ★ **Ask someone you haven't spoken to in a while.**
- ★ **If you have joined a new organization, ask the founding members and the newest members.**
- ★ **Finally, and most importantly, always, always, ALWAYS ask someone who intimidates you.**

You never quite know how you're perceived until you ask! This then empowers you to raise the bar to the next level!

POSTURE 03 : *PASSION* FOR OTHERS

Who Do YOU Say I Am?

Use this listing to ask 10 people what they think about you.

Do this often! The most important feedback you can receive is feedback that helps you grow. The goal is not to find praise. Ask respondents how you can be *better*!

10 People Whose Feedback I Value	
(Person Number 1's Name)	(Relationship)
(Person Number 2's Name)	(Relationship)
(Person Number 3's Name)	(Relationship)
(Person Number 4's Name)	(Relationship)
(Person Number 5's Name)	(Relationship)

HUMILITY

(Person Number 6's Name) (Relationship)

(Person Number 7's Name) (Relationship)

(Person Number 8's Name) (Relationship)

(Person Number 9's Name) (Relationship)

(Person Number 10's Name) (Relationship)

POSTURE 03 : *PASSION* FOR OTHERS

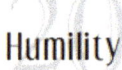
Humility

"
I Will HONOR My Mentors!
"

Mentoring is easily one of the most exciting opportunities in the world! Who wouldn't want to *lovingly* impart EXPERTISE about life, love and the pursuit of happiness to an eager listening ear for an extended period of time?!**EXACTLY!** EVERYONE wants this cherished opportunity, so for ALL who have been blessed to carry the title *mentor*:

KUDOS TO YOU for A Job Well Done!!!

Mentors are EVERYTHING! You confide in them. You learn from them, and you LOVE them for being cherished models in life! Mentors make you better! They willingly show you the ropes and commonly enable you to skip some steps where you might otherwise slip up. Mentors make life a tad bit easier because they support you when you fall and they encourage you where you lack—they help you to believe in yourself! What has your mentor done for you lately? Thank them for it ALL! Honor them however you can!

Affirmation Journal

★ **How have my mentors helped me over the years?**

1.

2.

3.

4.

5.

HUMILITY

★ **How do I honor my mentors?**

*I am not a teacher,
but an awakener.*

ROBERT FROST

POSTURE 03 : *PASSION* FOR OTHERS

21 Humility

" # I Will Value SELF-EXAMINATION! "

In putting yourself in the BEST position to move forward within the realms of GREATNESS, it's always in your best interest to not only quiet yourself enough to *listen* to others, but to also go to necessary lengths to continuously solicit the *feedback* of others. The hope is that you come across actionable input that propels you to *be* and to *do* better as an individual and also as a leader within your respective roles and communities.

Without proper input from all relevant sources, self-examinations are lacking. Soul-searching self-examination have benefits that will far exceed the common thoughts you have about yourself no matter their frequency. Introspection requires time, adequate input and willingness to break the molds in order to find viable resolutions. Profitable self-examination is an unceasing process. New information is readily applied to find further insight while building onto foundations that have already laid over time.

Affirmation Journal

★ **When did I last conduct a thorough self-examination?**

_____
_____
_____

★ **What factors should I consider during introspection?**

_____
_____
_____

★ **How frequently will I commit to self-examination?**

_____
_____
_____

Say Aloud: **I Will Value Constant Self-Examination!**

Humility

> ## I Will HUMBLE Myself!

"We have not because we ask not!"

That is a fact! The most basic things you could EVER ask for are often just immediately beyond your awareness *or* they are beyond your acceptance. Many times, you can *see* exactly what you desire—you perceive it, yet you are blind to asking and even more blind to receiving! You limit yourself by your own lack of humility, acceptance and appreciation!

GET OUT OF YOUR OWN WAY!!!!

Sometimes, you have NOTHING because you ask NOTHING of those right beside you!

Affirmation Journal

★ **What am I standing in the way of?**

_____

_____

_____

_____

★ **What am I asking for without being humble to receive?**

_____

_____

_____

_____

Be a master of giving and receiving! Be a master of *getting out of your own way* long enough to get what you've desired all along. BE HUMBLE!

Humble yourself enough to do something that makes you proud!

A great man is always willing to be little.

RALPH WALDO EMERSON

23 Humility

> # I Will HONOR My Parents!

To honor your parents is to accept them for who *they* are and to also appreciate them for who *you* are. Honor your parents—not simply in thanks for what they've done for you but also in acknowledgment for their help in shaping you into the individual that you've become. Thank them through your efforts, in your successes and with the recognition that you were created as a product of their own personal encounters with life.

In love, and with sincere gratitude for your life, always embrace the utmost joy in consideration of showing your parents the honor due them. Whether they be good or bad parents, rich or poor parents, alive or with you no more, parents are to you a great many things. They are life-givers, and for this, you owe them your ALL.

Affirmation Journal

★ **In what ways do I show honor to my parents?**

_____
_____
_____
_____
_____
_____
_____

★ **Why do my parents deserve honor?**

_____
_____
_____
_____
_____
_____
_____

HUMILITY

★ **How could I better show honor to my parents?**

_____
_____
_____
_____
_____
_____
_____
_____

Say Aloud: I Will Honor My Parents!

POSTURE 03 : PASSION FOR OTHERS

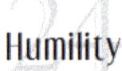

Humility

" I Will Look to Others for HELP! "

No one ever said that success is a journey to be taken alone! Don't be afraid to ask for help! Find at least one person around you, whom you respect—a person who silently motivates you—and ask that person for HELP!!! If you can't find someone to depend on, you will NOT succeed because at the very least, you must *first* be able to depend on yourself!

Don't make the foul decision to be invariably self-sufficient. You *may* believe that self-sufficiency is a prided characteristic of culture, race, gender, generation and related groups. While independence *is* a grand trait to possess, being too self-reliant can produce stagnancy, stubbornness and pride. Without the inclusion of outside input, you will find yourself backed up against a wall not knowing *how* to ask for help when you *need* it MOST! *(TRUST ME on this one!!!)* In other instances, you will ask for help and have absolutely NO clue how to use it! Make a commitment NOW to learn the value in asking for and *receiving* help!!!

Say Aloud: I Will Look to Others for Help! I Will Receive Well!

It is unwise to be too sure of one's own wisdom.
It is healthy to be reminded that the strongest might weaken
and the wisest might err.

MAHATMA GANDHI

Journal Prompt...

On my journey, I am asking for _____

_____

In my life, I think about HUGE goals like _____

_____

AND… I Will Look to Others for Help!

Humility

> # I WILL LISTEN!

Many people suffer greatly from the disease of closing out the thoughts and ideas of others *and* also from feeling the need to constantly vocalize our own. Everyone wants to do ALL the talking—no one wants to stop and listen.

One main component of listening is that you must first learn to quiet yourself so that you're in the best position to fully hear and comprehend. This isn't to say that you shouldn't vocalize your interests—beyond simply expressing ourselves, you must exercise wisdom in timing and presentation of feedback.

Self-empowerment involves more than just *self*. It requires the inclusion of people and processes within our environment. Others may have very valuable things to express to you, so don't be afraid to seek out, *and* respect, the input of another. Without listening to those around you and paying attention to your environment, you won't be readily able to position yourself for greatest impact.

Affirmation Journal

★ **In what areas of my life can I stand to do more listening?**

★ **Besides people, what other things should I listen to?**

★ **How can I learn to quiet myself and listen better?**

Say Aloud: **I Will Change! I Will Listen and Maximize Impact!**

Humility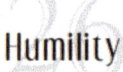

> ## I Will LISTEN with My WHOLE Heart!

Listening isn't a characteristic that should ever be taken lightly because it's your looking glass into the world. You listen with your ears, your eyes and the rest of your senses. Anyone seeking to be a grossly effective listener learns to also listen with their heart.

Bringing your heart into the equation makes use of the listening senses all the more impactful. When you listen with your heart, you not only listen to hear, but you listen to lead and impact change within *any* situation. Pure hearts are the best listeners, so it's recommended that you listen to *understand* versus merely listening to *respond*. Pure listening ears should be impartial and without judgment, seeking nothing more than clarity and understanding. Come from a place of openness, integrity and wisdom as you tend to the thoughts of others.

Affirmation Journal

★ What does it mean to listen with my heart?

★ What can I gain from life by listening more thoroughly?

Say Aloud: I Will Listen Thoroughly, with My Whole Heart!

The best listeners listen between the lines.

NINA MALKIN

JournalPrompt...

Do I listen to others?
How does this help me or hurt me?

_____
_____
_____
_____

Do the people around me share their insight, input, and advice?
How does this help me or hurt me?

_____
_____
_____
_____

How does listening to others help my process?

_____
_____
_____
_____

What does listening provide to me that other things won't?

_____
_____
_____
_____

How does humility connect with the affirmation: *I Will Listen with My Whole Heart!*

_____
_____
_____

POSTURE 03 : *PASSION* FOR OTHERS

Humility

> # I Will Consistently Support an Entrepreneur!

Many lack the desire and good sense needed to consistently support others in joy and humility. Some wrongly feel that others must be *deserving* of support or that they must *do* something widely "impressive" for support to be justified. Don't sit on the sidelines justifying your own lack of action! Non-supportive people are all too ready to lend a listening ear when other people fail because of... YOU GUESSED IT: Lack of Support! **What a world!**

Entrepreneurs DESERVE your support! Entrepreneurs DESERVE for you to show how proud you are of them for boldly venturing out on their own. They deserve it, not because someone says so, but because they NEED it!

Just the same as anyone else, courageous people need to be reminded that someone cares! They need pats on the back the same as anyone else, if not MORE so! It gets lonely at the top! That's a fact.

Don't allow the entrepreneurs around you to feel lonely. Show them just how proud you are by supporting them through whatever means you can.

Affirmation Journal

★ Which entrepreneurs within my network make me proud?

1. _____
2. _____
3. _____
4. _____
5. _____
6. _____
7. _____
8. _____
9. _____

Do they know that I am proud of them? _____

_____

HUMILITY

★ How have I shown them my support in the past?

★ How can I regularly show them my support in the future?

Humility

> ## I Will Consistently Support a Worthy Cause!

Ever-changing attitudes dictate the persons, products and platforms that people will—and will not—support. If people won't support each other, what then, will they do? How will they encourage not only the person or platform in question, but how will this behavior encourage more leaders to venture out with their own products and platforms?

Support others because their causes deserve it! Their courage deserves it. *They* deserve it and *you* deserve it! Your measures of support have far-reaching implications for the future of society, for your communities and for your family. Furthermore, the support you show to others facilitates lasting feelings of goodness within.

Who have you supported lately?

Affirmation Journal

★ What worthy cause have I supported lately? Why?

★ What worthy cause would I like to support? Why?

HUMILITY

★ What do my personal contributions do for these causes?

★ What do my contributions to these causes do for me?

Say Aloud: I Will Consistently Support a Worthy Cause!

*When I do good, I feel good.
When I do bad, I feel bad.
That's my religion.*

ABRAHAM LINCOLN

Humility

> # I Will CHERISH Growth!

Life gives you hurdles. Life gives you *many* hurdles. With these hurdles come pain, loss and disappointment. You *will* cry at times—it hurts, but you live to see another day!

Unfortunately, you might sometimes find yourself repeating the same experiences multiple times. You miss the message anytime our pain is too unbearable for you to self-reflect. You miss the message when you work *around* situations instead of working *through* them. You miss the message each time you deny the existence of a problem and your role within its solution *and* cause.

Don't continue to miss messages. Take ownership of issues and face them HEAD-ON!

Though the hurt and burdens are yours to bear, there is growth potential within each and every moment. Cherish that growth! You face HUGE frustration if you find yourself repeating the toughest lessons. Your happiness isn't worth losing because of your lack of actionable awareness, so be present in EVERY moment! Look forward to the growth that even pain can bring.

Say Aloud: I Will Cherish Growth! I Will Be Actionably Aware!

Journal Prompt...

In the midst of my hurdles, how can I practice reminding myself to cherish growth?

What will be the ultimate outcome of this practice?

Humility

> ## I Will Be BETTER!

Say Aloud: **I Will Be Better! I Will Make Personal Progress!**

Some people LOVE to join in the ebb and flow of political debates and social movements. Some LOVE to passionately participate in the *current* current events! People throw around lofty statements regarding what needs to be done to do *this* and changed about *that* within our world, within our society or even within our dying solar system!!! Some people take joy in fighting for, or *against*, movements that have absolutely NOTHING to do with them! **NOTHING!**

The BEST place to start movements for social betterment is *within*! If YOU want to change something, start first with *yourself*! Don't sit back and wait for a willing example of progressive stewardship—be your own example! While you may not always be able to immediately evoke change in life, you *will* always be able to aggressively change yourself!

Say Aloud: **I Will Be Better! I Will Change NOW!**

Change Your Posture! Change Your LIFE!

Don't wish it were easier.
Wish you were better.

JIM ROHN

Journal Prompt...
What does the following quote mean to me? *I Will Be Better!*

What will I do to celebrate my personal progress on a regular basis?

POSTURE 03 : *PASSION* FOR OTHERS

Humility

"

I Will Be HUMBLE!

"

You can travel many places in life yet you go NOWHERE if you travel without humility. You could accomplish a great number of goals yet you accomplish NOTHING without humility. You may transcend awareness of varied thought yet you know NOTHING without humility.

Do you gain *anything* out of this world if humility doesn't accompany you along the way? What have you gained without humility as the reward? NOTHING!

You are NOTHING without humility in your firm grasp!

Never place yourself above anyone but *yourself*! You are only better than the person that YOU were yesterday. Aspire to be as great as YOUR fullest potential—once you arrive at the top, consider yourself above no one. Keep yourself mentally aware of the process that you underwent to embrace the life that you have. Remember the most humbling experiences of your life, and let those be remind you of your humanity—of your kinship with those who are still on their own personal journey to greatness.

Say Aloud: I Will Be Humble! I Will Reach FULL Potential!

*On the highest throne in the world,
we still sit only on our own bottom.*

MICHEL DE MONTAIGNE

Journal Prompt...

Throughout this process, what 5 things have I learned about humility?

1. ⎯⎯⎯
2. ⎯⎯⎯
3. ⎯⎯⎯
4. ⎯⎯⎯
5. ⎯⎯⎯

What will I do with what I have learned?

but wait! there's more!

Additional reader-only content including worksheets, workbooks, writing prompts and journals can be found at www.Change-Your-Posture.com. Visit us for resources on this book and others within the Change Your Posture series.

I would LOVE to personally connect with you!

Attn: Coach D Nicole!

Sh'Shares NETWORK

1601-1 N Main St 13202

Jacksonville, FL 32206

www.Change-Your-Posture.com

www.CoachDNicole.com

www.ShShares.com

Send book praise and reading group pictures to:

SHINE@Change-Your-Posture.com

It is my sincere prayer that you were blessed by the contents of this book. I look forward to securing our connection well into the future!

Thank you for your GREATNESS!

Coach D Nicole is a very charming and spirited first-class professional who is passionate about encouraging, supporting and coaching others within their personal lives and business endeavors. As a transformational life coach, she is most loved for her wit, boisterous personality, direct and upfront coaching style, and generous, authentic smile!